T-ball Is Our Game

By Leila Boyle Gemme

Photographs by Richard Marshall

 CHILDRENS PRESS, CHICAGO

For Ellen and Abby, the rest of the team

The pictures in this book were taken in the
Wilshire Park District of Los Angeles, California.

Library of Congress Cataloging in Publication Data

Gemme, Leila Boyle.
   T-ball is our game.

   SUMMARY: A group of youngsters learn to play
T-Ball. Includes the rules for the game.
   1.   T-ball—Juvenile literature.   [1.   T-ball]
I.   Marshall, Richard.   II.   Title.
GV881.5.B68   796.357'8   77-17273
ISBN 0-516-03630-0

11 R 93 92

We play T-Ball.
There is no pitcher
in our game.

We hit from this tee.

Our coach teaches us how to play.

We learn to hit.

A good hit gives you a good feeling.

We learn to catch.

We learn to throw.

15

We learn to run.

18

We have to watch the batter carefully.

We get team shirts for our games.

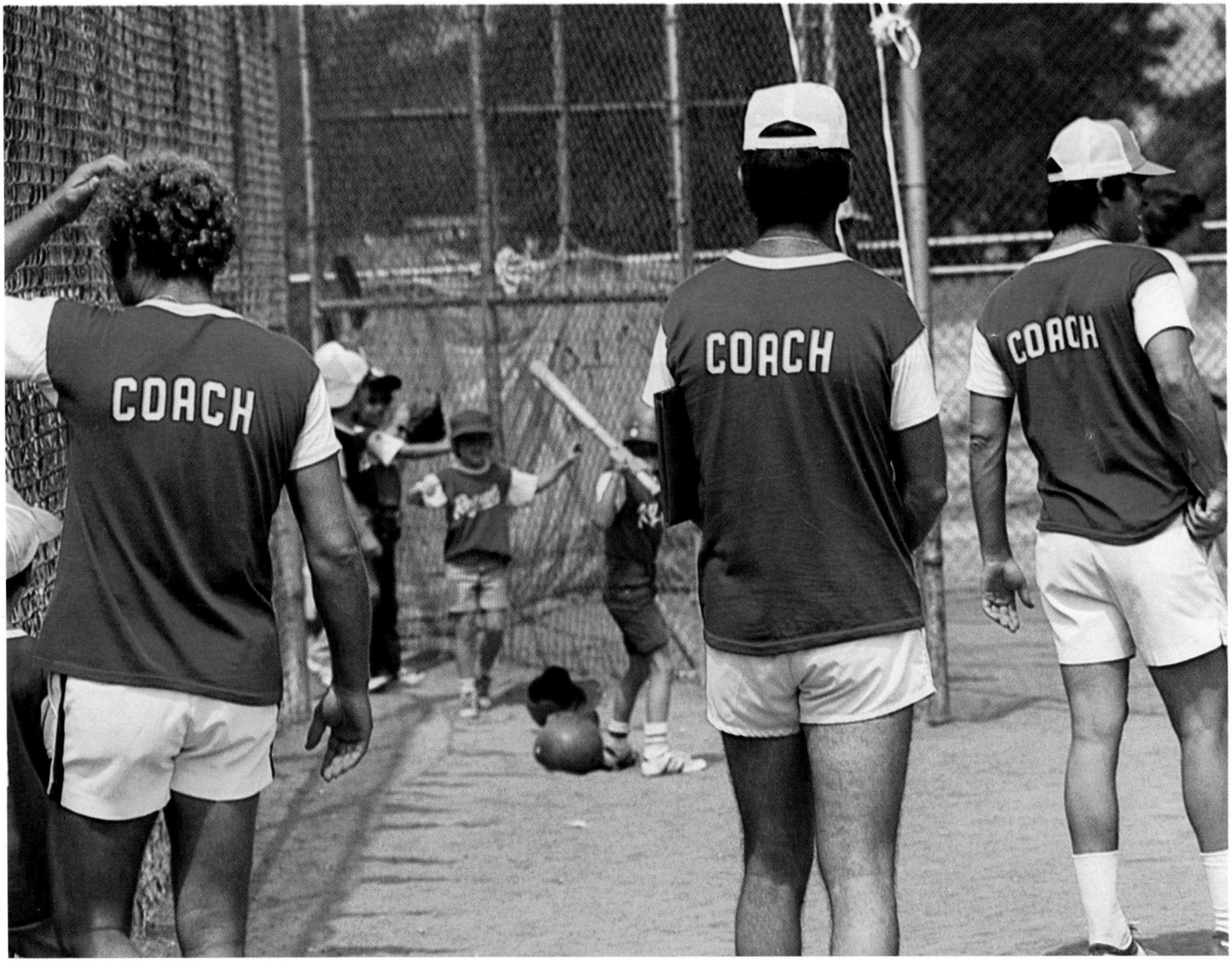
COACH
COACH
COACH

Our coaches get team shirts, too.

Sometimes we get worried.

Often we win.

Sometimes
we lose.

We always cheer the other team.

And we always have fun,
because T-Ball is our game.

Rules for T-Ball

1. T-Ball is a game played by boys and girls in the first and second grades. It uses baseball's rules but makes some changes in those rules.

2. T-Ball teams can have as few as nine players. They can have as many as seventeen players.

3. T-Ball games last six innings.

4. There is no pitcher in T-Ball. Players hit the ball from a pole called a "tee."

5. Batters must hit the ball cleanly. If the bat hits the tee, it is a foul ball. This counts as a strike.

6. The ball must be hit out of the batter's box. Balls that are hit off the tee and stay inside the batter's box are foul balls.

7. If a team makes three outs or gets ten runs in one inning, then its turn at bat is over.

8. In the last inning, the ten-run rule does not count. Each team gets to make as many runs as it can until three players are out.

9. A player who throws the bat is out.

10. When a ball is hit to the outfield, a fielder throws it to the infield. When the ball reaches the infield, play must stop. The runners may not run to any more bases. This is true even if the ball is not caught by an infield player.

About the Author

Leila Boyle Gemme was a high school teacher for several years before turning to writing. "When my children were born, I needed an 'at-home' career, and writing seemed like a good idea," she explains. Her lively household in Winnetka, Illinois, includes a husband, three children, and a dog. The subjects of her works are varied. Among other things, she has written about the sports world, entertainers, and the space program.